The Wit and Wisdom of
Highland Cows

This is a STAR FIRE book created for LOMOND

STAR FIRE BOOKS
Crabtree Hall, Crabtree Lane
Fulham, London SW6 6TY
United Kingdom

www.star-fire.co.uk

First published 2007

11 10

3 5 7 9 10 8 6 4

Star Fire is part of The Foundry Creative Media Company Limited

The CIP record for this book is available from the British Library.

ISBN: 978 1 84204 128 4

Printed in China

Thanks to: Cat ETaylor, Andy Frostick, Sara Robson,
Gemma Walters and Nick Wells

The Wit and Wisdom of
Highland Cows

Ulysses Brave

LOMOND

Foreword

For years I studied Zen and the Art of
Animal Self-consciousness. Subsequently I
have written a large number of management,
self-help and philosophical texts over the
years, which have provided helpful advice
to those less fortunate than myself.
Here then, is my latest offering.

Ulysses Brave

Inner calm is a rare, often unrecognized quality.

*Celebrate your difference
from the crowd, take pride
in yourself.*

Sometimes it seems as though everyone is against you. Try to find the reason before taking it personally.

DO NOT
GRAB
HAMISH
BY THE
HORNS

Try to take the long view
of your life.

If you need to stand and fight, make sure you're ready to lose for your cause.

The invisible barriers
which surround us all seem
to appear when we least
expect them. Don't give up!
There may be other ways to
your achieve your goals.

While the nurture versus nature debate still rages, remember to be kind and loving to your children and friends. Even if you have to whisper!

*Don't forget to appreciate
what you have.*

Sometimes, the grass
really is greener on
the other side.

*Take a rest between meals
and contemplate the good
fortune of your surroundings.*

If the tide goes out on your luck, make sure you're still standing in the same place, to benefit from its eventual return.

Zen-like one-eyed looking can be useful when trying to see beyond the immediately obvious.

If fate seems bewildering,
remember that your future
is, at least in part, in your
own hands.

Management manuals often refer to "decision drivers" and "drilling down". These can be useful tools for even the most basic tasks in life.

Romantic love can be hugely life-enhancing.

Try to perfect an ironic tilt of the head. Any angle between 3° and 5° will work well.

Caught between a rock and a hard place, always choose the rock. At least you will know what it looks like.

When dreaming it can be
useful to observe your own
multiple personalities of Self.

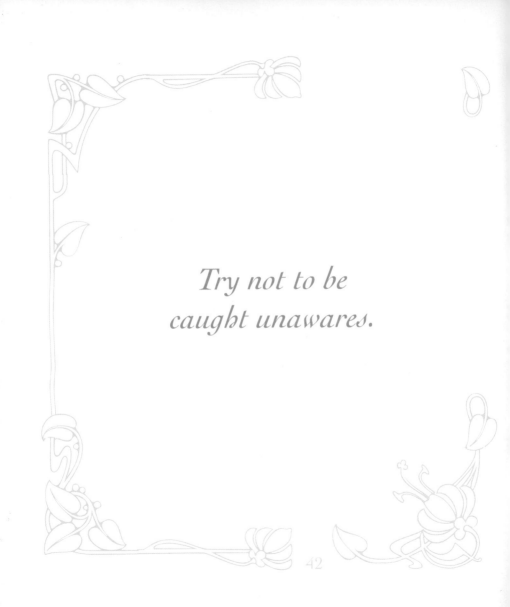

Try not to be
caught unawares.

*When in repose, try to
find ways of strengthening the
muscles around your mouth.
This will provide hours of
entertainment in later life.*

Remember, don't allow yourself to be treated like a number. You are a beautiful being, with needs and desires of your own.

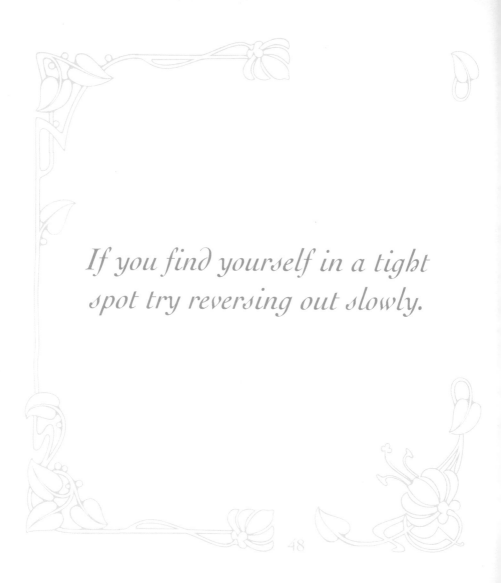

If you find yourself in a tight spot try reversing out slowly.

Try to break the vicious circle by stopping occasionally and rethinking your plan.

Sometimes our own shadow
can come to life and offer
support and guidance in
difficult times.

If it all gets too much for you, try going to a quiet place and shouting as loud and long as you can.

Being leader of the pack
isn't always about adulation
and reward.

Always lift your head high
and be proud of yourself.

Try to look beyond your emotional barriers. Sometimes you have to leave behind friendships that were forged under different circumstances.

If you're stuck in a rut, try to lower your expectations to see life from a different perspective.

Sometimes burying your head to avoid a problem is the only option.

*As we grow older, we behave
in ways that were once
regarded as unacceptable.
Now we either don't know what
we're doing, or we don't care!*

Take care with exercise.
It can generate some
unpleasant symptoms.

*Ah, just enjoy that early
morning snack. You must
fortify yourself for the
busy day ahead.*

See you soon ...